How to Dance as the Roof Caves In

poems

Nick Lantz

GRAYWOLF PRESS

This publication is made possible, in part, by the voters of Minnesota through a Minnesota State Arts Board Operating Support grant, thanks to a legislative appropriation from the arts and cultural heritage fund, and through grants from the National Endowment for the Arts and the Wells Fargo Foundation Minnesota. Significant support has also been provided by Target, the McKnight Foundation, Amazon.com, and other generous contributions from foundations, corporations, and individuals. To these organizations and individuals we offer our heartfelt thanks.

Published by Graywolf Press
250 Third Avenue North, Suite 600
Minneapolis, Minnesota 55401

www.graywolfpress.org

Published in the United States of America

ISBN 978-1-55597-670-5

2 4 6 8 9 7 5 3 1
First Graywolf Printing, 2014

Library of Congress Control Number: 2013946926

Cover design: Jeenee Lee Design

Cover photo © Corbis

For Vicky

Contents

I

Conversation in Which Neither of Us Speaks

OK, yes, I'm in love
with the sentence, the dependent

clause like a pale toe sticking out
from under a blanket. That toe,

your toe, has more to say
about the universe
than I could in a lifetime

of poems. To say you
are under the blanket
is insufficient. What

could be sufficient? The official
kilogram, a platinum-iridium cylinder

stored in a vault in France, has lost
the weight
of a fingerprint, and what

looks like an hour
can chew off my tongue.

Whole lives go mute
in the waiting room, the voice

eroded by fluorescent
light and antiseptic.

Though scientists
cannot bring themselves
to say

lost. Instead,
they say *relative change.*
They say, *a discrepancy
of mass,* and when I was

cleaning out your old office,
I found a sheet of paper
scarred

from where you'd tried
and tried to revive

an inkless pen. Now the rain
interrogates the roof,

and the house's gutters
spill their guts, confessing

each refugee leaf
they've sheltered since winter, and already

I'm telling lies
about you,

because all I'm left with
is this sentence
that I love.

How to Travel Alone

The same painting is hanging on all four walls
of my hotel room: Ship at sea.
       Ship at sea.

Ship at sea. Ship at sea.

An empty bed won't say
I love you
until its jaw falls off. The rain believes
the earth exists

just to give it something
to fall against. What can I do

from my dingy little room but close
the blinds and turn up the TV?

Some days I come out wrinkled like a jacket
exhumed from a suitcase. Some days

I'm as constant as the last soggy corn flake
at the bottom of a bowl of milk,
that piece that keeps giving

the spoon the slip. I'm that ship that can't
find shore, can't be sunk.

Just days without you and I've got
that midnight streetlight tan,
that Big Chug Jug caffeine carelessness, that one loose
toll booth tooth, these highway hiccups.

The wooden benches in the train station
remind me of the pews in the clapboard church

where my cousins are still swaying
with the holy spirit. Oh, ship at sea, they sing, you are
          my ark, my raft.

But where is the cross, the portrait of Jesus knocking
on the inn door? All we have is the schedule board,

its clattering
numbers and letters, the clock that chimes and chimes.

As pigeons descend to devour
a dropped sandwich,

the station agent's voice echoes over
the PA speakers: Here is my ham on rye, with whom
I am well pleased.

I write postcards I don't
send. Each one
is a confession.
I eat microwaved cheeseburgers until my stomach

rocks and pitches like a ship at sea.
Your voice on this cell phone is a bug
trapped in a jar. Your voice on this phone
is a sliver under my fingernail.

How many nights will you be staying with us?
Here is your key card. Here is a brochure
to help you interpret the stains

on the ceiling tile, to augur the roaches
and broken glass. Do not be alarmed if you hear

a shout, a trumpet. The high school band
tournament is this weekend.

Your signal faded. Your call dropped.
I can't find my reservation number.

Your voice on this phone is like a ship at
Never mind, I found it.

Meanwhile, the greasy clouds go sliding around
on the sky
like gray eggs in a skillet. Meanwhile,

the laundromat beauty queens
in their wash-day sweatsuits thumb quarter

after quarter into the machines
and pray for miracles. Meanwhile, a shut-in dies buried
under a collection

of snow globes of Paris, where tiny couples walk
up and down the Champs-Élysées in endless winter.

A stranger in mirrored shades says Take off
your shoes, take off your jacket.

I do, I do. I unthread my belt in one long pull
that whispers it from its loops.

Will a skycap please bring a wheelchair to Gate 7B?
Jennifer H_____, please call your sister
in North Carolina. Roger M_____, Roger M_____,

please return to the security checkpoint
to retrieve a lost item.

Board by zone number. Sit in the wrong seat
just to meet a stranger, to apologize, to say

My mistake. You're breaking up. If the engines fail, don't worry:

on our cell phones, we'll watch
live footage of our plane fireballing
into the ocean, our own
bodies bobbing in the wreckage and surf.

Look, that's us waving.

I write postcards I don't send. They all start
Dear ship at sea . . .

When I stop to throw
them into a dumpster, I glance down

into that darkness and see the continent where I was born, as if
from space, its cities lit
like clustered stars.

There are only two directions in the map
of my life: the way to you, and the way
from you.

Fork with Two Tines Pushed Together

It's fast and cool as running water, the way we forget
the names of friends with whom we talked and talked
the long drives up and down the coast.

I say *I love* and *I love* and *I love*. However, the window
will not close. However, the hawk searches
for its nest after a storm. However, the discarded
nail longs to hide its nakedness inside the tire.

Somewhere in Cleveland or Tempe, a pillow
still smells like M____'s hair.
In a bus station, a child is staring
at L___'s rabbit tattoo. I've bartered everything
to keep from doing my soul's paperwork.

Here is a partial list of artifacts:
mirror, belt, half-finished 1040 form (married, filing jointly), mateless
walkie-talkie, two blonde eyelashes, set of acrylic paints with all the red
and yellow used up, buck knife, dog collar, camping tent (sleeps two), slivers
of cut-up credit cards, ashtray in the shape of a naked woman, pen with
teeth marks, bottom half of two-piece bathing suit, pill bottles containing
unfinished courses of antibiotics, bank statements with the account number
blacked out, maps of London, maps of Dubuque, sweatshirts with the mas-
cots of colleges I didn't attend, flash cards for Spanish verbs (*querer, perder,
olvidar*), Canadian pocket change, fork with two tines pushed together.

One night, riding the train home from the city,
will I see a familiar face across from me? How many times
will I ask Is it you? before I realize
it's my own reflection in the window?

Forgetfulness means to be full
of forgetting, a glass

overflowing with cool water, though I'd always
thought of it as the empty pocket

where the hand finds
nothing: no keys, no ticket, no change.

After the Lightning Strikes, Count

It is the window you sit by that scrawls
the exact shape of your longing on you. Love is all

afterimage, ghost
of a lightning bolt haunting the retina,
headlights swarming you

as you walk the shoulder of the highway
between your house and hers.

             The imprint of your jacket,
the seam of chest and arm, jagged in her cheek.

Change the window,
        and you forget the deliberations
of hawks and rabbits, the soft elbow of road
that showed through the trees. Now all you care for

is the retarded teenager in a green smock
sweeping the sidewalk outside the corner market,
how he appears

on the hour, a bird emerging
from a cuckoo clock.

Three years later, another window, and now
you sit to watch the tide's
        retreat, men in waders
digging clams, the sound of their shovels biting mud
drifting up to you across the bay.

When you close your eyes, you see her,
a pale carp surfacing in a murky pond.

What do you call the flinty part of you that misses
winter, which here is only rain?

Every morning the bed sheets are curled in imitation
of the body
that has left them behind.

The clouds tick by like beads on an abacus.
The halyard keens and keens against the flagpole.

Re: 5 ways to enhance your love more passinnate

—Spam email subject headings

1. Your time for enhancing has come

Sharp, professional, and honest
    Your health
    Your happiness
No Study Needed
Low Education? Don't Worry, now You can BUY

New potent formula requires one dosage
    Car loan
    School loan
    House loan
    Debt loan
Specially delivered naked

If your wife needs your attention, you can help her

2. We are respected for quality and reliability

Public debt
Government debt
Credit card debt
Paving debt
Oxygen debt
Debt consolidation loans bad credit

    Yes, locks
11 ladies are online now

Discover your true size
    Turn a small knob into a huge wand
    Put Godzilla's manhood to shame

How do I get out of debt?

3. i am looking for you

Maria is online now, waiting for you
Nadia is online now, waiting for you
Katrina is online now, waiting for you
        Adjustable rate mortgage now available
        Bling-bling now available

Every locker room will envy you

Is it you nicklantz
Call me now nicklantz
Where are you, Nicklantz

4. Still single?

Suffering from low self-esteme?
Wish you looked like Appolo in bed?
        Like a pocket elephant in your pants
        Your trunk has shrunk?

Get the most for your money here.
Join millions who have achieved their size

Don't suffer in silence in the bedroom
        Touch your ladys soul
        Drive her insane with pleasure
        Lay her out and take what you want

Make all girls heat

        Four lenders want to talk to you
Killer discounts
Debt insurance
Car refinance
Mortgage amortization
        No girl can be a dead fish after this

Are you ready for us?

5. Trying to reach you one last time

Its time to increase your head
Climb the corporate ladder now
Insert more health into your life
CheapWatches from $192
        Cartier, Bulova, Rolex

Bags . . . cheap
RX DRUGS . . . CHEAP
New . . . Arts and Crafts dining in solid American cherry

The principle of traction

Advantages of micro-vacuum pumping

A gentlemen is jugded by his size

URGENT message re: your 401k
Your internet access is going to get suspended
Your health care will be terminated
Your checking account will be closed

Which lender will you choose?
Your wife need your attention?
Want to have fantastic nights?
Painkillers?
        Its me. Is it you?

How to Help a Ghost

Some days I leave the grocery store and walk
all the way to the door
of our old house without thinking. Even the strange
dog waiting at the window seems to recognize me
as I stop just short
of trying my key at the lock.

You were a thread of cobweb I breathed in and couldn't
swallow, couldn't cough up. All our boxed-up letters
can't fathom the indifference
of the garbage truck, hoisting
the cans like an aging bodybuilder.

Hell is a country where it rains year round
and you must spend all day writing postcards
to relatives you don't love. Today, you write,
it rained.

And wasn't it the rain that caught you
rushing between buildings, someone else's jacket
on your back, face turned
away, as if to avoid a camera? I wasn't

there to see it, but I imagine all the things
you never told me as a line of footprints
dried into the concrete.

My mistakes are throwing
bunches of roses at me, cheering
for an encore. So here is my aria: a dirt
road, seven beers, the headlights
off. Enough of this.

Some day, one of the dark shapes wandering
across the frozen lake will turn out
to be you. I can already hear you at the door
shaking the frost
off your boots.

Hawk and Rabbit

A hawk nested on the roof of your building,
and for six years every
poem you wrote, every kiss you gave

your wife, was a rabbit that either escaped
into the hedges or died in the air.

Millipedes are born and die by the thousands
on the laundry room floor and never dream
of the moon. The book's spine is broken

out of love. The trumpet sings
with borrowed lungs.

You could try bending the mended wheel, weeping
tears of milk. Jesus won't appear twirling
a sword like a baton.

To wit, the overturned garbage can,
locks of hair swept
across the barber's floor, the crow whose head
swivels like a closed-circuit camera.

The bus-stop shaman claims man has not one
soul but many. A soul
for drinking wine. A soul for kissing,
for laughing. A soul for taking out

the garbage. A soul for peeling apples
at the sink, for losing
utility bills. A soul for writing checks.
A soul for doing
nothing. A soul for sucking a blackberry-stained finger
until the stain is gone.

Carbon from all of the burned books is born again
in the mustaches of generals and the long ears
of rabbits. If you can hear

the tremor of the neighbors' daughter
practicing her violin, count
yourself lucky. The world's oldest

musical instrument is a flute carved
from a vulture's leg bone.

Though it is more correct not to say *oldest*
but *oldest surviving*.

Can you imagine: those lips? that throat? that music?

You see a truck with "James Tate Plumbing"
stenciled on its side panel, and you imagine
the eponymous plumber
elbow deep in a drain, coming up not with a fist

of hair but snow globes of Pompeii, the jawbone
of an ass, the endless red ribbon
of a rabbit's intestine, the half-darkness

of our bedroom when
the shades are drawn.

Origami

Start with a blanket. It should be a hospital
blanket, that threadbare white
of sickness. Start with a PICC line, threaded
from your arm up deep into your chest.

Start with what has been cut out of you.
Start with what you don't say as you grow thinner.

No. Scratch that. Start with the gable of a house
where swallows have built a nest. Start with the hose
you use to blast them out.

Start with the fingernails that one day just
come off. You must begin folding. One edge
must meet the other. The cleaner the work
at the beginning, the more lifelike.

Start with the word predisposed. *Pre,* for before. As in,
years before you were born someone
on a beach dipped a finger in a tide pool
and muddied the water. From *disposer*: to arrange, order,
control. To place. One edge, the other. Your body
the fold in the middle.

How to Tour the Historic Battlefield

1.

A witness tree is a tree that lived
during the battle, and today one of the rings
deep inside its trunk is still tangy with gun smoke.

If you peeled me like an apple,
would you find

our argument that I walked around
for days, a pilgrim perambulating
some holy relic, waiting for it to transform

him? Would you find the dinner
when a friend, drunk on wine, said how kind

we were, and you and I looked
at one another, and all the unkind things
we'd ever said or done hung

between us, a single strand
of spider silk, visible
only from a certain angle?

2.

In the gift shop they sell walking sticks
made from trees
cleared from the battlefield. They sell

recreations of Confederate currency, candles
shaped like cannons, bullets on which you can pay
to have your name inscribed.

Outside the Visitors Center and Museum,
we run into a group of students
from a university where they aren't allowed

to date people
of a different color. They are posing
by a statue of Lincoln, but Honest Abe doesn't look

affronted. All day, Honest Abe
bears the rabbit ears
that teenagers thrust up behind his head. He bears

the red-white-and-blue popsicles dropped
in his lap. After all, doesn't his dull bronze skin blaze

in the spot on his cheek where thousands of people
have kissed him?

3.

The side of the bus says *Dramatized in Living Stereo!*
and you lean in and whisper to me,

Isn't everything?

Oh, it would be something to ride the bus
of my own body while a man on a PA
rattled off the trivia of my life. On the left

is his first marriage, which is being restored
through your generous donations.

But no such luck.

4.

This battle happened because ten roads
converged here. This battle happened
because both armies were following

a rumor of a warehouse of boots.
This battle happened because a very, very long time ago,
one person

put his naked foot on top of another
person's head
and said I am more than you.

It's difficult
sometimes to get the facts straight.
Did the free black woman escape

her captors and hide in a church belfry
for three days

while below

doctors and carpenters
and anyone
who could wield a saw

amputated the limbs
of the wounded, wounded who just kept

coming, until there was nothing
to do but throw the severed

arms and legs out the windows?

When you and I see
the man taking
a picture of the Virginia monument and wearing
a shirt that says *If at first you don't
secede, try, try again,* do we shoot him
a nasty look? Or do we say
nothing, and trundle back
on the bus?

Years ago, when I said In that case, I don't. Not at all,
and for three days
we didn't speak,

who was the first to break that silence
like a gunshot?

5.

As we pass a cemetery,
the tour guide tells a story
about a young man who left

a career as a composer
to join the army,

only to be shot dead
in the first hours of the battle. On your left,
says the guide, is his grave. People say if you stand
beside it at night, you can hear him decomposing.

What a laugh this gets. You laugh,
I laugh, the whole bus laughs,
the bulldozers that are plowing

houses to restore the battlefield
to its period state
stop to laugh and laugh.

6.

That night, we'll make bread
in the kitchen, watching

in the dark window
the ghostly couple making bread
in their kitchen.

What must their lives
be like, we wonder? To work side by side
without speaking, like a scene cut

from a silent movie? Though isn't there something
in the way one hands a bowl
to the other, the way they dance

around each other in that
narrow space?

We think of poor Jennie Wade, killed
by a stray bullet that passed through two closed doors
and found the Mason-Dixon

of her spine. And to top it all off, her name
was Ginnie, not Jennie,
though some reporter

got it wrong, and now the house
where she died is the Jennie Wade House,
and at the restaurant

where they serve nineteenth-century food
in period clothing and tap water in pewter goblets
while fiddle music plays
from a speaker hidden in the ceiling,

the bread they serve is also called Jennie Wade
because Ginnie died
with a loaf of bread in her hands.

To Paint Lightning

You must begin with something lost, a scrap
of paper, a cell phone burrowed

between the cushions, thrumming
      like a mouse. You must start
      with regret, its orbit

      elliptical, reeling years deep
into forgetfulness but still
tethered to the hot, heavy center.

Begin with a Ganges of longing, holy
and so polluted one sip
      might kill you.

Make the footpath connecting
the two lovers' houses

a temple. Let the path of a bird circling
      a field describe the dome.
The waves of kudzu its walls.

Begin with the moonlight
wobbly on the water. The word
the mind gropes for and never finds.

Here are the thoughts that crack
the temple apart: your grandfather's boots

standing empty in the basement,
the shopping cart clattering
      up and down the sidewalk at 3 a.m.,

the burglars bowing on the doorstep,

the firefly, who draws its mate
not with light but with the intervals
of darkness.

On the Lake Path at Night You Look

down: the ground, writhing.
Little toads, or frogs (who can tell?).
None bigger than your thumbnail.
But hundreds, multitudes, moving.
You stand there, afraid of what another
step might do. Try not to think
of the steps that brought you here
through the runny moonlight, what
you have already destroyed.
Tomorrow a gull will carry the discarded
ends of your sandwich to its nest.
Even now the mosquitoes
coalescing around you like an aura
of hunger will feed the chirping bats.
There is your house, folded in the woods
like a splinter the flesh has grown
over but remembers with the slightest
pressure. There is the path that leads
to it. A window, gaping, golden.
And in the darkness where your hands
and feet are invisible, there is her voice,
and yours, speaking together.

II

How to Stage a Community

1. All of These Houses Are Empty

We were hired to park our car
in the driveway, to sit

at the window, to push a toothless mower
back and forth across a ragged lawn where just

the other day, a man in a truck had come
to spray paint the brown spots green.

It wasn't much. It wasn't even
a living. Our neighbors: out-of-work
actors, students,

a day laborer who didn't speak two words
of English. They all went about daily lives

that were not their lives, going out
to check the mailbox, to move the garbage can

to the curb, back
to the garage.

To be seen, that was the important thing.
The buyers might appear
at any moment, rare birds

or a comet not witnessed
for generations. They were meant to see us
and to think

I might live among such people.

The day laborer always waved to them, but we
watched, a pair of hired eyes

behind a borrowed window, as the agents led

the buyers into the empty
houses, like a pair of coins

vanishing under a magician's
silk handkerchief.

2. What Happened

to the people of Chichen Itza? I'll tell you.
Someone said Bubble. Someone said Underwater
mortgage. Someone said The great plumed serpent,
which is our currency, has flown away.

And their stock brokers threw themselves
into the deep cool of the cenotes,
and their priests wept tears sharp as flecks
of obsidian, and the jungle

surrounding their great pyramids shrugged,
and that shrug was the sound of the farmers
walking away from their fields

and never coming back. In hell there is a house
of teeth-chattering cold,
and a house of things that bite you in the darkness,
and a house of weeping razor blades, and just like that

we were pawning our KitchenAid Mixer and then leaving
most of our clothes in garbage bags
outside of Goodwill on a Monday morning
and then cutting up our credit cards and canceling
our cell phones, which we threw into a lake.

And then what we could neither give nor sell
we threw away until we were whittled down
to what would fit in the car, with room
for us and for the dog,
and then we left, and no, we haven't
joked about eating
the dog yet.

3. Recruits

We saw the flyer
in the lobby of the public library
and called the number from a payphone.

At dawn, we drove
to a vacant lot and met the staging supervisor,
who had gathered the other applicants
around an old shopping cart. Look,

he said, this is not fun. This is not
a normal job. But it has to be done.

So he led our caravan to the development,
a honeycomb of streets where nothing
moved. I thought of how when winter peels away
a tree's leaves you can see all of the nests
left abandoned in the upper limbs.

The staging supervisor stood in the middle
of the street. He pointed one way,
then the other. All empty, he said.
He explained the job. One woman

started weeping, softly, into her sleeve. Without
saying anything, she got into her car
and drove off. We all stood in silence

listening to the sound of that car
getting thinner and thinner like the edge
of a knife.

Well, said the supervisor,
now she knows something about herself.
And so do you.

4. Neighbors

We live in different houses every day
depending on which property the agents plan
to show. Today, our next-door neighbor
is a former day laborer. He shows us
his right hand—pinkie, ring, and middle
finger sheared off at the second
knuckle so it looks like he's always
pointing at something. Rototiller,
he says. A yard, choked with weeds,
weeds he should have cut and bagged
first, and knew it, but instead
he lined up the tiller at one corner
of the yard and just waded in.

He'd seen a tiller hit a buried stone
and leap into the air
like a startled cat, blades pinwheeling
in the sun. He'd seen a dog
that spent all morning barking at the tiller,
getting braver and braver until
it lost its nose. He'd seen a man
in frustration wrestling
the tiller backward over a tough patch
and tripping, the tiller climbing
up onto his shins. A lot can happen
quickly, and he knew it.

He got maybe fifteen feet before
the tiller seized up. Should have
turned it off. Better yet, he says,
should have climbed in my truck
and driven home right then.
The long grass was wound round
the blades, the axle, and—

he can't explain it to this day.

Maybe it was the heat, a giant's thumb
pressed between his shoulders.
Maybe somewhere someone was kissing
her sweetheart for the first time,
and this was how things balance
out. Maybe he was just stupid
and lazy and tired and all the other
names he'd curse himself with
over the next few weeks.

But he reached into that thicket
of blades and pulled
at those weeds. Pulled at them
as if they were pythons strangling
his own child, and when they came
loose, for an instant, he felt—

And then the blades came back
to life, and that was that.
He remembers tucking the hand
under his other arm, squeezing
it there while the owner of the house
called an ambulance, then her husband,
then her husband's lawyer,
and when it was clear
that he wasn't going to bleed out
there on the shaggy lawn,
she went inside and fixed
herself a drink, but he could
hear her through the open
window, talking on the phone, saying
This is just the last thing I need.

5. Buyers

The buyers all look like embedded journalists
in a war zone. The buyers never actually buy

anything, and we wonder about nomenclature.
Are we then still
owners? Are the dead still living?

They take pictures. They huddle together
and talk in whispers. They are mostly young

couples, looking for a deal, looking for a future
with a dotted line they can sign and initial.

Their clothes are rumpled
as if they just got dressed
after sex, as if they were just released

from a night in jail.

Somewhere on the other side
of town they have an apartment with extra

bedspreads and a food processor
and embroidered saffron napkins

they only bring out
when guests are visiting.

They keep a box of condoms tucked under
the bed. They argue quietly in the kitchen.

They have a list of baby names (Morgan,
Errol, Sean) but only their friends
are getting pregnant.

The agent leads them around
the side of a house to look at the trellis, the patio,
the blank spaces into which they might insert
their lives, and they look

like two trees about to be struck
by lightning.

6. Developments

From the highway you can see half-built
housing developments, the homes abandoned

in various states
of undress, all huddled around the cloudy mirror

of a manmade lake. Coming soon, says
the sign: Hidden Valley, Foxfire Valley, Valley

of Sorrows. Canada Geese zero in
as if some chemical in their hearts draws them

toward failure, and they settle
by the hundreds on the skinny silt shore,

on the wasted lawns, honking and shitting,
proclaiming their dominion. It is illegal

to kill them, to chase them off, so the development
company leases the land

to the university, and graduate students
come to sit in lawn chairs and jot notes

about group dynamics, sketch
nesting behavior and territorial displays.

One of the students has streaks of sunblock
on her face like warpaint. She is trying to prove

that the geese are not monogamous.
They're cheaters, she says, I just know it.

7. Bodhidharma

Our staging supervisor is an impatient monk.
You live here, he says, but you do not live here.
The lawn is your lawn, but it is not your lawn.

We try on his philosophies like a father's coat.
We plug in a phone that we know no one
will call. We eat out of boxes with our fingers.

In the seventh hell, there are creatures
like a verb turned inside out. If only we could
open these blinds and see a different street.

We are just spores napping in the breeze.
But the garbage, he says. Whatever garbage
you make, that's yours one hundred percent.

8. Jobs

One stager's job is to wash
his car all day, ten a.m.
to three p.m., seven days
a week. He starts at one
bumper, and when he gets
to the other, he starts
over again. He was chosen
because on the first day,
he arrived in the nicest car,
a 2003 Mustang. He makes
twice what we do, and at first,
we envied him. Now we pity
each swipe of his pus-yellow
sponge. We feel each spray
of the hose as an open
palm striking our cheeks.
A car can only get so clean,
he says. A man can only
get so broke. He jokes
that the coils of garden hose
looping across the drive
look just like his signature
on the bankruptcy papers.

9. Is There a Problem Here?

We sleep in our car. We learn where you can sleep in your car without any-
one bothering you about it. We make friends with raccoons and coyotes. We
name them Mrs. Salvage and Little Sassafras and Mr. Wastenotwantnot.
We cinch our belts. We eat ramen noodles dry. Truck stops. The parking
lot of the twenty-four-hour grocery store. One night at a time. We write
This is an adventure on our back window with soap. We write *Behold* and
Just divorced and our old, disconnected phone number, and we pray that it
still rings somewhere, that someone picks up and says Hello from inside a
kitchen that is noisy with laughter and wine and steam from a pot of pasta
just dumped in a sieve in the sink, and we think we can hear the water
dripping down into the basin and trickling into the dark pipes below the
house, deep into the earth where we must be living now because when
we wake up it is always dark and noisy and close, and the sound we think
is our hearts beating is just the sound of some security guard rapping his
knuckles on our window.

10. We Tell Our Friends We Went

on a staycation this year. The slide carousel
lurches from image to image. Here's a slide
of our living room carpet, worn by the door
and table. Here's a slide of the street seen hazy
through the kitchen window (the small dark
shape is a child on a bicycle who circled
the block all summer). Here are the fragments
of a satellite that rained in our yard: scorched
bits of metal as tender as a bird's breast bone.
Here the cricket who sat like a carnival barker
on the rain barrel and creaked out his pitch
to the neighborhood. Here the underside of a shoe
that never left the house. Here the loads
of dingy laundry piled like the dung of some
plodding pachyderm of commerce. Here the plums
rotting where they fell. Here the squirrel patrolling
the knife edge of the fence. Here the dog's eyes
watching it. Here the possum that invaded
through the dog door and hunched under the kitchen island,
creeping out to steal, bite by bite, from the bowl
of kibble. Here is the dog studiously avoiding
that part of the house. Here is the broom
with which we evicted the possum
from the premises. We sawed the handle
of that broom into three pieces
so we could fit it in the garbage can. We did this
with gloves on, late at night, our voices
pinned somewhere below
a superstitious whisper.

11. Not a Love Sonnet

Would you believe me if I told you
my heart is a modular home carried

on two tractor trailers
with Oversize Load signs

on the back? No, scratch
that. My heart is a dollhouse armoire

sold for twenty-five cents at a yard sale,
an estate sale, a foreclosure sale where ferocious

old ladies pick over the folding tables
of my life for something to keep

the boxes in their attics company,
something to send their grandchildren

who are moving to college but never call,
something to sell for a profit on eBay.

12. One Day, Ravenous, We Call the Pizza Hole

We don't deliver there, says the boy on the phone.
What do you mean? we say.
That neighborhood is well outside of the Green Zone, he says.
This isn't Baghdad, we say.
We deliver to Baghdad, he says. We have two franchises there.
We tell him he can go to hell.

Twenty minutes later, we call back.
Let us talk to your manager, we say.
He sighs. My manager made a delivery to your neighborhood last week,
    he says. He was
never heard from again. Now there's no one else. It's just me and the rats
    here.
This is a nice neighborhood, we say. An upstanding community.
Nice try, he says.

We call back.
You talk a big game for a delivery boy, we say.
In my basement, he says, I have ten thousand candles, canned food to last
    three months,
gallons of water and a filtration system that will make my own urine
    drinkable.
But can you call that living? we say. We can hear him shrug—it sounds
    like a stone
falling down a hole without making a sound.
What will you read? we say.
Instruction manuals, he says. Takeout menus. My own name, so I don't
    forget it.

We call back.
What would Jesus do? we say.
I have transcended the puerility of dogma, he says.
Come on, we say, be a mensch.
I had a dream, he says, in which I was a worm boring my way through
    the heartwood of the world.

Dreams are the random firings of synapses in the brain, we say. Like
    birds startled from a tree. Don't worry about it.

We call back.
We say, Tell us your name at least.
Our name is Legion, he says, for we are many.
My name is mud, he says.
My name is a palindrome, he says. A palimpsest, a riddle, a bad joke.

We call back.
We'll tip you ten, we say.
No way, he says.
Fifteen, we say.
OK, he says.

13. Plausible

We wonder if the buyers find it suspicious
that we are home watering our lawns

and walking the dog in the middle
of the afternoon, in the middle of the week.

One of the out-of-work actors asks
our staging supervisor if we should come and go
as if we have jobs. Real jobs, he says.

Another asks if maybe the development
company can set us up with fake jobs, fake offices
with fake mold issues in the duct work,

fake desks where we can pretend
to sit, pretend to work. Wouldn't that, he says,

make the illusion complete?
Don't get cute with me, says our supervisor.

The world of suffering, he says, is an illusion,
a pillowcase full of bees.

We ask what a pillowcase full of bees is, what
it has to do with anything. You take things

too literally, he says. We think he may be right.
We think he may have been drinking, but we don't
say anything.

I think about plausibility, how at ten,
when my father drove me the twenty miles

to school each morning we passed a paper mill,
its stacks of flatulent smoke, and every

morning I asked my father what the place
was, and he said A cloud factory, and I

believed him.

14. Jobs

When our friends ask what we're doing for work these day, we say
>We work in existential real estate.
>
>We curate a postmodern art gallery.
>
>We're personal assistants to Grigori Potemkin.
>
>We're impersonating people with bad credit scores.
>
>We are disciples of a spiritual community.
>
>We throw things against the wall and see what sticks.
>
>We spit-ball.
>
>We brainstorm.

We say, you know the cracks people fall through?
>We're the crack regulators, we keep
>
>those cracks up to code.

15. Recipe

Someone suggests roadkill. To eat? we say.
Why not. He shrugs, and the shrug smells
like fur matted with blood. It smells not like
the way your mother used to hit you
with a rolled up *Cosmo* when you were too
loud, but like your father seeing and not
saying anything about it. You cook anything
long enough, you can choke it down.

16. You Are a Recessionista

and I am a thriftifarian. I rake a stack of leaves
in the yard and say: civilization!
In bed, we page through coupon books as foreplay.
We are buying whatever is on sale. We buy strawberries
that make you break out in hives, and we eat them,
oh yes, we eat them. We eat
the Burst Bubble Breakfast Special
at the local diner, though it is the same raft of bacon
and wet sneeze of eggs that it was a year ago and the year
before that. We're all about homedulging
and bleisure. We stuff the dog bed with shredded
bills, and when the dog sighs and turns
in its sleep, we hear our future, a tiger
rustling in the grass.

17. Education

Here is what I've learned: what Mrs. Melton
taught us about cursive in third grade was true. It won't
make a difference. Of course

that's not what she meant to teach us, coming in
every day with her thermos full of coffee and a fresh booklet
of animal stickers. We admired the lace

of her lessons whispering across the chalkboard.
That wasn't it. It was when we saw her
on weekends, at the mall, selling women's

handbags from a kiosk by the food court. It wasn't
even a real store. And my god when she saw us
and smiled in that way, well that
was more than we ever wanted
to know.

18. Thieves

One night, a house is stripped
from the inside, all the fixtures
pried out, drywall bashed open
to get at the copper pipes.

Our staging supervisor lines us up
the next morning for a lecture.
It is so early we see a coyote
slinking down the street

toward the culvert, toward
the woods, toward whatever burrow
or nest of matted grass he calls
home. The light in his fur

is fringed with gold. Greedy,
says our supervisor. He thinks
it was one of us, but can't prove
anything. Greedy, he says again.

19. Haunted

At the bar one evening,
one of the out-of-work actors says these houses
are haunted. The owner, he says, left a pair

of salt and pepper shakers. Ceramic. Shaped
like bantam roosters.

I put them in a drawer, he says, but
the next day
there they were

strutting on the counter top. Now I don't touch
anything, he says.

He is joking, of course. He has been practicing
this story all summer, the story
in which everything is a joke.

My glass is haunted by the ghost
of my last drink, he says and raises the glass so that light
seems to pour into it.

We tell him
Emily Dickinson said that art is a house
that tries to be haunted. He writes this down
on his cocktail napkin.

Someone suggests another
round. My wallet, he says,
is haunted by the ghosts of dollar bills.

The out-of-work actors all live together
in a one-room apartment, and we imagine them sleeping
together, a ball of garter snakes in a cave,
trying to stay warm.

After last call, they weave down the block singing
until their voices are swallowed up
by a siren, by a howling dog, by someone closer by
saying If she won't come, I'll do it, I'll fucking do it.

We don't tell anyone we hear voices
in the water that chokes out of the faucet.

We don't mention the strange fingerprints
on the window. We don't mention the credit card
frozen in a cup of ice in the freezer.

We don't mention the dark smudge
at the bottom of the door jamb where for years

a cat rubbed its body on its daily patrols.
We don't tell anyone about the faded blue
dress we found hanging

from a hook on the back of a bathroom door, smelling
as if someone's grandmother

had just stepped out of it. We don't

tell anyone that when the concrete
in the basement was poured, someone got down
on her hands and knees

while the floor was still soft
and left her imprint there at the dark root
of the house that we haunt by day.

III

How to Appreciate Inorganic Matter

As I clip my toenails, one foot propped
on the garbage can, I think of all the cruel teeth of dinosaurs
that have shrunk
so slowly into the bills of ducks and finches.

Your father, by the time I met him,
was nothing more
than a work shirt draped over a ladderback chair, a tyrant
with all the tyranny siphoned out.

In his kitchen, he kept cocking his head
to catch the ring of a phone
that wasn't ringing.

He showed me a windowless room
with a piano, played a little Joplin rag, and couldn't remember
my name.

It was later, on the hotel bed, TV muted, that you said
He used to take me in that room and push
the piano against the door so I couldn't
get out.

Life is chalk dust on your sleeve and satellites failing
in their orbits, the gallons
of milk still in the unchewed grass, a cassette tape
on which your childhood self tells a story.

Which is to say when you see a man in coveralls
you ball your fist. Which is to say
that the hair we had as children
has all been cut

and swept away, and our skin
and bones, and every atom in our hearts
has been replaced now many times over,
and yet jazz sets your teeth together
like millstones,

and a crater filled with a beautiful lake
is still a crater.

We didn't see your father again. We checked out
of the hotel with the little red light
on the phone

still blinking, and only later wondered
if the next occupant
would pick up that phone, thinking the message

was for him, and hear your father rambling on
about leftovers in the fridge, the neighborhood boys
he can't tell apart, or how all day he sweeps
his driveway, how the leaves, those goddamn leaves,
keep falling.

Four Reasons You Don't Write the Letter

1.

After the summer of hands
on each other's skin, the summer you knocked her up,
the summer of breathing into the phone
when she asked What do we do?, the summer she miscarried,
or didn't, the summer she vanished, the summer you
were suspected, the summer of accusing letters
from her mother, the summer of not driving down to the 7-Eleven
to smoke in the parking lot with your friends,
the summer every thought of her was a sparrow trapped
in the garage:
        after that, what could you do?

2.

Lightning is a love
letter writing itself on the same tree
over and over, until there is only cinder. It never
remembers what it meant
to say, the reason, only
        the preamble: listen, listen, will you just listen to me?

3.

If only every morning arrived
like a 747's tires shrieking onto the tarmac. Instead, days
go by like ants pouring
out of a crack in the kitchen wall.

No, not days: years. Loading pallets
        in a warehouse, driving a backhoe until its arm
was your own, pushing a broom, eating ham and cheese by yourself
on the curb out back, fighting nausea when you woke at dawn,
inspecting apples, bailing hay, restocking vending machines,
throwing newspapers, selling drugs, sleeping with the window

open in winter, stripping siding, waking up with a bloody nose,
coaxing splinters of fiberglass from your palm, fire spotting
from a stand in the forest, dozing in a toll booth, driving
a pickup up and down the fire roads, teaching children how
to build a fire, how to extinguish one, wondering if one
of those faces resembles yours but knowing
        they are too young, too happy.

The coyotes that howl all night are only asking What
does your pillow smell like? Does your shoulder still ache
where her face burned itself into you?
How many pictures of her are boxed in the attic?

4.

Somewhere she is drinking iced tea with her eyes closed.
Somewhere she is bagging groceries and living in a trailer.
Somewhere she is married to a man who lost
a hand to a roadside bomb and counts
        himself lucky.
Somewhere she thinks about you every time
        she sees a man sweating through his shirt.
Somewhere she doesn't remember your name.

Somewhere she is the scraps of a rowboat washed to shore
        after a storm.
Somewhere she is the question the water asks

then retracts, then
asks again.

Help

—a found poem

How to Sit at a Computer
How to Smile
How to Reach a Consensus
How to Remove Bloodstains from Clothing
How to Love Learning about Things
How to Tell People You're Keeping Your Maiden Name
How to Call Bolivia
How to Believe in God
How to Make a Wedding Toast

How to Survive without Cooking
How to Enjoy Arizona All Year Long
How to Treat Dehydration
How to Get Rid of Black Circles under Your Eyes
How to Avoid Marriage and Other Committed Relationships
How to Choose a Wedding Chapel in Gatlinburg, Tennessee
How Not to Always Talk about the Same Things

How to Ignore People
How to Find Cat Urine with a UV Light
5+ Tips for Boiling Water
How to Stop Comparing Yourself to Others
How to Control Perfectionism

How to Buy Cruelty-Free Makeup
How to Practice Nonviolent Communication
How to Win a Street Fight
How to Stop Being Needy

How to Be Popular
How to Be Confident
How to Be Attractive
How to Make a Meal Plan for One

How to Be Your Own Valentine
How to Buy Tablecloths for Your Wedding
How to Choose a Pencil
5+ Reasons You're a Control Freak

How to Perform Self-Hypnosis
How to Survive a Freestyle Rap Battle
How to Escape Materialism and Find Happiness
How to Live on Minimum Wage
How to Raise Your Leg up to Your Head
How to Survive Federal Prison
How to Survive a Fall through Ice
How to Call in Sick When You Just Need a Day Off
How to Detect Lies
How to Have a Perfect Marriage

How to Do Nothing
How to Buy Nothing
How to Be Thankful
How to Be Busy
How to Relax When Relaxation Techniques Don't Work
How to Do It Yourself
How to Stop Excuses
How to Recognize a Manipulative or Controlling Relationship
How to Know When You're Hungry

Symptomatic

Doctor, my heart is a crumpled
beer can. If you listen at my chest
you can hear the pull-tab
rattling.

All these years I've been holding in the same lungful
of smoke I inhaled behind the 7-Eleven
in seventh grade. When I open
my high school yearbook, everyone
in the pictures turns their backs to me.

Doctor, my childhood was a bomb crater
in the middle of a cornfield.
My mother was a lapsed tornado. My father, an abandoned
oil derrick. That was his name, Derrick. No joke.

All my dreams are Doppler weather maps
of west central Illinois. My love life is a town so small
you'll miss it
if you blink while driving through.

My mind is a twelve-story
parking garage, and I've forgotten
where I parked my car. Doctor, I know that when I find it,
I'll have locked my keys inside.

Once I saw my neighbor cut his dog's ear off
with a pair of scissors
after the dog had shit on his porch.
My neighbor went inside, and the dog sat
on the sidewalk, until another dog came up
and licked the place where its ear had been.

How to Dance When You Do Not Know How to Dance

You and I fit together
like two millstones, and oh the music

we make of grist, going round
and round the same

arguments (taxes, laundry,
the leaky

faucet, the unremarkable
disasters of marriage).

My feet are two ugly badgers
that hide their faces

in the dirt when they see
clouds tip-toeing

above the lake.
The homely trees in winter
crack and fall

into one another: that is how I must
look to you as I gather

dirty plates to the sink.
You say Talk to me about

the weather. I say that once
a tornado carried

a birdcage with a live canary inside
a quarter mile, the cage
flying, the bird flying

inside of it. I don't know how
to make the faucet

hold back its drip. I try
to open a bottle of wine

and half the cork breaks off
inside the neck. But you, Love,
you ignore

the flecks of cork floating
in your glass, the way

I teeter and reach out a hand
for something that isn't there.

Love, I will mate the limp socks. I will fold

the shirts so their sleeves
wrap around their flat,

empty chests. I will drip words
into your ear as you fall asleep.

I will carry boxes up and down
the basement steps all day.

I will pour another glass of wine,
and we will dance the slick sidewalk two-step,

the lassoed-calf flop,
the chain-gang shuffle, the all-thumbs

jitterbug,
the fish-out-of-water jive.

After Seeing a 400-Year-Old Basket in the Museum of Natural History

Don't think of a childhood of unrequited
          bread crusts, a youth
of eviscerated candy wrappers

blowing down the street in a manner not unlike leaves.

The rinds, socks worn through
at toe and heel, balloons that gave up

your stale breath years ago, apples with one brown bite
missing. A great, bristling

sandbar of cigarette butts in the middle
of the Willamette. The condoms, the favorite shirt forgotten
on a stranger's bedroom floor.

The crook of an arm your head occupied
for seven winters' worth of cold nights.
The mouths that used to

say your name and now
don't, the pillow and mattress
rebounding from your indentations, the grass springing back

even as you lift your foot.

          There, over the edge of the field, are the skins
that you walked out of, flake

by flake, reassembled and lit from within
like rice paper lanterns at an autumn festival.

How to Properly Fold and Insert a Letter into an Envelope

All the forest fires start
with some poor sap burning

love letters in an abandoned
campsite.

Maybe while he's driving away
from the ashes he thought he put out,
he thinks about his body falling away

like a spent booster rocket as he roars
out of some self-made crater.

You and I would be burning the world by the acre
if not for the intervention of the door
that I close behind me to keep
from being cruel, the valve of a heart that keeps
the blood flowing
in one direction.

When we are silent, that silence is an empty parking lot
visible from space.

I get up early, you go to bed late.
You cultivate orchids that resemble discarded

wedding dresses. Those orchids fold

and unfold themselves. They do not throw magazines
at the wall. They don't refuse to look you in the eye.

In the Atlantic Ocean, there is a nuclear submarine,
and in that submarine is a safe. And inside that safe

is another safe. And inside that
is a sealed envelope.

And in that envelope is a handwritten letter telling
the submarine commander
what to do if his homeland is burned

to a cinder. Some days, I don't know
whether I wish I were the submarine, the commander,
or that letter. Some days, yes,

I wish I were the ashes of the homeland.

At night the smoke detector in our apartment
goes off for no reason. And who remembers
what I said
or what you said? When we wake

to its shrill proclamations, it's only
us, standing in our worn-out underwear, scared
then laughing.

After You Taped Your Chest X-Ray to the Window

Buy a boat. Christen it *The Pathetic Fallacy*.
Learn from the barnacle how to surrender

your attachments.

Admire the bitten apple, the way the kingfisher
commits its body to the water like a man falling

in love. When you pass a Laundromat
while walking home from a poetry reading,

stop to look inside at the teenage girl
face down asleep in her math workbook

as the rows of fluorescent lights burn
apocalyptically above her.

The slow ruination of a life is a thin broth
you ladle spoon by spoon
                    out of a cast-iron pot.

Repeat after me: I was born a pushpin in a box
of paperclips, a pointing finger

in a land of bent knees.

You can think open the stones. Think the rain
drop by dizzy drop. Think

the bar of soap bobbing
in the tub. Think the drunken winter sun.

Go sit in some quiet place

and memorize the faces of the passing
ants as they slowly dismantle

a discarded apple core. Be as glad
as the speckled woodpecker

as he bashes his head against the tree. Yes,
some days your mind will come out

matted like the back of a dog that has spent
all day digging through the brambles
                        and the rain.

But last, and this is important,

you must pour all your sweetest honey
                        into a shallow bowl and then,
                        without hesitating,
dip your finger into it.

How to Forgive a Promise Breaker

That winter all our friends' marriages were cars
entombed by snow plows. Our families, their toes
in the Pacific, don't understand how something
can be buried, how you can do nothing but wait,

see what's left after the thaw. He moved out,
but she stayed until he stopped paying rent,
and then the sheriff knocking the way police
knock—like a shovel banging the outside

of your casket—and then her things in bags
and loose heaps on the curb, calling us, calling
anyone who would pick up the phone. We have
a few boxes of her books in our closet, brought

them with us across the country when she didn't
return our calls—what were we supposed to do?
Probably a box of vases wrapped in spare linens
has made its way to a basement in Memphis,

her LPs in someone's trunk in Albuquerque.
A stack of high school yearbooks, a gym bag
full of shoes. The cat her sister took in and paid
five hundred dollars to cure of kidney disease

before it died crossing the road a week later.
And her, she's buried somewhere, not literally,
but lost as one of those cars you might recognize
by its bright red antenna ball poking out of the snow

like a poppy, the blinking light on your
cell phone, the message that says Please just
take some of these things off my hands while I
sort this out, just a few weeks, I promise, I swear.

The Chisel

Each time a boat dips its oar into the water, Venice sinks
    a little lower. It isn't the oar's fault.

        It isn't the crocodile's fault
that his teeth cross like the fingers of two hands clasped
in prayer. Hunger was Augustine's sin too, every time
he said Not yet, Lord.

In a museum, someone has collected
photo postcards

of lynchings. In one, the body is so small
among the gathered crowd
that someone has drawn an arrow

pointing to it. In another, a man stands
just off camera,
        propping up the dead man's head

with a stick.

In the nearly frozen river, the eagles will fish all winter.
At the last instant
before they sweep their claws
through the water, they look away.

        But don't mistake this

for remorse. The regrets of those eagles
can be measured with a teaspoon.

My dog sniffs the air where a tree has been
cut down, and then turns to look at me
                as if I am responsible
for the world of missing things.

A spider bites my thigh, but that bite
is a storm on the surface of Jupiter,

and I think of how often
Michelangelo must have stopped his carving
to kiss the thighs of David.

Loyalties

You can never say enough about the hinge
of the python's jaw or the nostrils of the shaggy bear

or how the mouse's ribs bend
to slide him through a crack. But what

of your wife, who is now across town, reading
a play about a woman who kills her own

children to take revenge on her husband?
Is the problem with love

poems, as a teacher once told you,
that you must decide if you're loyal

to the love or to the poem? Because the truth
is, yes, years before you met

your wife you were trysting with books
behind the high school gymnasium. You kept

a small notebook folded in your back pocket
the way other boys kept a condom

in their wallets. Those boys were scrawling
their lives on a different sort of blank page,

and somehow you came to believe that love
isn't something you can write about

unless it's ugly, or caustic as a mouthful
of bleach. In the poems, you and your wife

are always throttling your marriage
like the neck of some animal you want

to eat, but the truth is that your worst
argument could hide its face under a grain of salt.

The truth is that on your long walks,
when you reach some bend in the path and turn

toward home, you feel her as a comet
must feel the planet that it circles

once a lifetime, the way a pilgrim
kneeling in a reliquary feels the presence

of the beloved saint's finger bone
shrouded in velvet inside its gilded box. The truth

is that after a day apart from her
your hands feel as if they've been severed

and surgically reattached. That your heart
is a knot tied in a broken shoelace.

The truth, the terrifying truth, is that for her
you would dig a hole, and bury

that notebook in it, and then scrape
every line of poetry from the wall of your brain.

Ways of Beginning

Start with the scar bisecting   your father's back.
Start with air
          tangling through birch leaves
along the shore of Butte Lake, the dream in which you find
an infant inside a suitcase,

the way fog insinuates itself   across the bay,
the dust from Utah still on your clothes in Wisconsin.

. . .

Mallarmé told Degas that poems were made
of words,   not ideas, but yesterday
a thirteen-year-old boy dropped
          a block of concrete
off an overpass, killing
a woman as she drove home   from the movies.

      In the Atlantic, a shark conceived
immaculately.   On an island in Greece,
vultures dropped

          the bones of sheep off a cliff
to crack them open for the marrow.
      All of your mother's friends have cancer.

. . .

Even these words are a bridge collapsing
under the weight of a single pilgrim.

. . .

Pliny recounts the story of a woman sentenced
to be famished to death: her daughter,
a new mother herself, visited every day,

        and every day the jailer stripped her
to find the food she meant to smuggle in.
                              Until one day
she was discovered nursing her mother
with the milk of her own breasts.

Pliny calls this *piety*.

. . .

Even in their silent imitation of angels,
the monks of Cluny spoke with their hands:

for the sign of assent, for refusal, for quickness,
for a feast day, for dressing, for an old man, for talking, hearing,
for a keeper of donkeys, a knife, a needle, bread,
                For the sign of something bad, place your fingers spread
                out on your face and pretend that it is the claw of a bird
                grasping and tearing at something,
for sleeves, a gardener, eggs, fish (squid, lamprey, sturgeon, pike, trout),
for water, a book, the cup that holds the daily allowance of wine,
for mustard seed, a shallow bowl, blanket, belt, comb, hymnal,
                For the sign of a secular book that some pagan composed,
                add to the aforesaid general sign for book that you touch
                your ear with your finger, just as a dog usually does when
                scratching with his foot, because a person without faith
                deserves to be compared with such an animal,
for an apostle, a martyr, a man who speaks another language,
for not knowing, for undressing, a tunic,
for a flat dish, for kissing, for something good, for telling a lie,
for raw millet, for cheese tarts, for milk, for honey
                (Stick out your tongue for a moment and touch your
                fingers with it, as though you want to lick them).

There was no sign for God.

. . .

Start with long-lost twins

reunited on afternoon talk shows. Start with the sweetness
of honey, the heft of a stone,
        fog beading in your lover's hair.

Start with the glow   of the midnight TV
on an empty armchair.
                        Start with the angels,
who are mute   and therefore terrifying,
like glaciers,   like an expressway seen
from space, like a carcinoma,
                        like a block
of concrete dropping, almost slowly, out of the sky.

. . .

Inside the old sawmills, through the dust and screaming
of the gang saws, the sawyer could say this with his hands
        Start. Stop. Slow. Fast. How thick the cut, and how many.

But that was all: a world so cramped and loud
needed little else. What would have been the use

of describing the aria of the band saws, the sound
a blade made when it found a nail, a piece of gravel,

and shattered,
                the way a man's hand could vanish
if he leaned too close?   What good

would it have done to describe the heated mill pond
steaming on December mornings,
                                    the songs
of the pikemen working,   coaxing the logs
onto the jackslip. And what of the vast lots

where the finished lumber was left
to dry, stacks high and square as buildings
                    with boulevards between them?

Day and night that lumber sweated off
its moisture, and if you walked
                                those streets,
the smell was resinous and sweeter than any forest.

If such a word exists, start with that.

Acknowledgments

Many thanks to those who published earlier versions of these poems (sometimes under different titles).

Catch Up
"After the Lightning Strikes, Count"

Columbia Poetry Review
"How to Travel Alone" and "To Paint Lightning"

Connotation Press: An Online Artifact
"The Chisel," "Symptomatic," and "After You Taped Your Chest X-Ray to the Window"

FIELD
"How to Appreciate Inorganic Matter" and "After Seeing a 400-Year-Old Basket in the Museum of Natural History"

Harpur Palate
"Hawk and Rabbit," "How to Properly Fold and Insert a Letter into an Envelope," and "On the Lake Path at Night You Look"

Indiana Review
"Ways of Beginning"

Iron Horse Literary Review
"Four Reasons You Don't Write the Letter"

Michigan Quarterly Review
"Conversation in Which Neither of Us Speaks" and "Origami"

Milwaukee Shepherd Express
"How to Help a Ghost"

The Rumpus
"How to Dance When You Do Not Know How to Dance"

The Seattle Review
"How to Stage a Community"

Nick Lantz is the author of two previous books: *We Don't Know We Don't Know* (Graywolf Press, 2010), which won the Bread Loaf Writers' Conference Bakeless Prize, the Great Lakes Colleges Association New Writers Award, and the Larry Levis Reading Prize, and *The Lightning That Strikes the Neighbors' House* (University of Wisconsin Press, 2010), which won the Felix Pollak Prize. He lives in Huntsville, Texas, where he teaches at Sam Houston State University.

Book design by Connie Kuhnz. Composition by BookMobile Design & Digital Publisher Services, Minneapolis, Minnesota. Manufactured by Versa Press on acid-free, 30 percent postconsumer wastepaper.